GIANNIS ANTETOKOUNMPO

SPORTS SUPERSTARS

BY ALLAN MOREY

BELLWETHER MEDIA · MINNEAPOLIS, MN

Torque brims with excitement perfect for thrill-seekers of all kinds. Discover daring survival skills, explore uncharted worlds, and marvel at mighty engines and extreme sports. In *Torque* books, anything can happen. Are you ready?

This edition first published in 2023 by Bellwether Media, Inc.

No part of this publication may be reproduced in whole or in part without written permission of the publisher. For information regarding permission, write to Bellwether Media, Inc., Attention: Permissions Department, 6012 Blue Circle Drive, Minnetonka, MN 55343.

Library of Congress Cataloging-in-Publication Data

LC record for Giannis Antetokounmpo available at: https://lccn.loc.gov/2022050044

Text copyright © 2023 by Bellwether Media, Inc. TORQUE and associated logos are trademarks and/or registered trademarks of Bellwether Media, Inc.

Editor: Rebecca Sabelko   Designer: Josh Brink

Printed in the United States of America, North Mankato, MN.

TABLE OF CONTENTS

BUZZER BEATER!	4
WHO IS GIANNIS ANTETOKOUNMPO?	6
GETTING INTO THE GAME	8
A SUPERSTAR	14
LOOKING TO THE FUTURE	20
GLOSSARY	22
TO LEARN MORE	23
INDEX	24

BUZZER BEATER!

The Milwaukee Bucks are down by one point. There are seconds left in the game. Giannis Antetokounmpo gets the ball. The New York Knicks keep him from driving to the basket. Antetokounmpo must make a move. He goes up for a shot.

The ball drops through the net as the buzzer sounds. The Bucks win the game with a buzzer beater!

WHO IS GIANNIS ANTETOKOUNMPO?

Giannis Antetokounmpo plays in the **National Basketball Association** (NBA). He is a **power forward** for the Milwaukee Bucks.

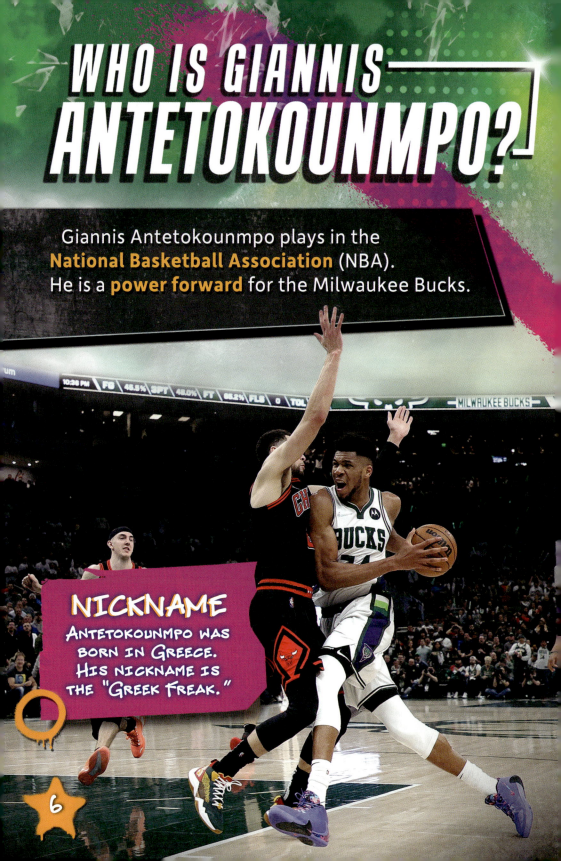

NICKNAME
Antetokounmpo was born in Greece. His nickname is the "Greek Freak."

6

GIANNIS ANTETOKOUNMPO

BIRTHDAY December 6, 1994

HOMETOWN Athens, Greece

POSITION power forward

HEIGHT 6 feet 11 inches

DRAFTED Milwaukee Bucks in the 1st round (15th overall) of the 2013 NBA Draft

Antetokounmpo is known for his size, strength, and speed. He is one of the NBA's best **defenders**. He often leads the Bucks in **rebounds** and **blocks**. He is also the team's all-time top scorer.

7

GETTING INTO THE GAME

Antetokounmpo grew up in Greece. But his parents are from Nigeria. They moved to Europe in hopes of finding a safer home. His parents struggled to find work and feed their family. Antetokounmpo often worked to help get food for the family.

Soccer Family

Antetokounmpo's father was a soccer player in Nigeria. His brother Francis also played soccer.

FAVORITES

FOOTBALL TEAM

Green Bay Packers

FOOD

french fries

COLOR

black

ACTOR

Will Smith

As a child, Antetokounmpo loved to play soccer. He hoped to be a star soccer player one day.

When Antetokounmpo was 13, a coach for the local basketball **club** saw him. The coach wanted Antetokounmpo to play for the club. The coach promised to give his family money if he played.

ANTETOKOUNMPO FAMILY

At first, Antetokounmpo struggled to play basketball. He could hardly **dribble** the ball. But he practiced hard to make the team.

In 2011, Antetokounmpo began to play for one of the club's higher-level teams. During one game, Antetokounmpo scored 50 points. He was on his way to becoming a basketball star!

12

BASKETBALL BROTHERS

Two of Antetokounmpo's brothers, Kostas and Thanasis, also play in the NBA.

Antetokounmpo was a teenager. But people began to notice his basketball skills. People from the NBA traveled to Greece to watch him.

A SUPERSTAR

Antetokounmpo was 18 during the 2013 NBA **Draft**. Teams thought he still needed to work on his basketball skills. But they also saw he had a lot of talent.

2013 NBA DRAFT

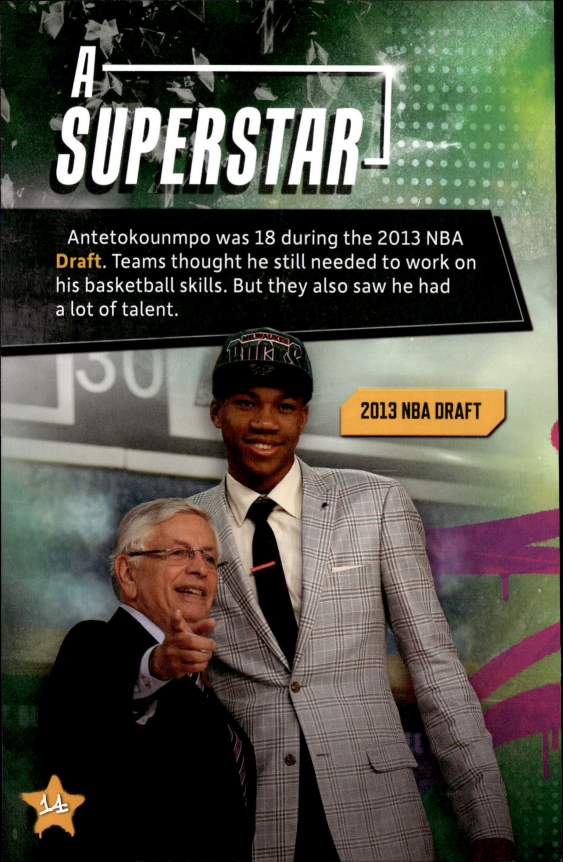

GIANNIS ANTETOKOUNMPO MAP

- Greece National Team, Athens, Greece — 2014 to 2019, 2022 to present
- Milwaukee Bucks, Milwaukee, Wisconsin — 2013 to present

The Milwaukee Bucks took a chance on Antetokounmpo. He was their first-round pick. During his **rookie** year, the Bucks had the worst record in the NBA.

During the 2016–2017 season, Antetokounmpo was voted Most Improved Player. He led the Bucks in rebounds and blocks. He was also the team's top scorer.

The next season, Antetokounmpo played in the **All-Star Game** for the first time. In the 2018–2019 season, he was voted the NBA's **Most Valuable Player** (MVP).

2018 NBA ALL-STAR GAME

During the 2019–2020 season, Antetokounmpo was awarded NBA MVP again. That season, he also won Defensive Player of the Year honors.

Antetokounmpo had another successful season in 2020–2021. He led the Bucks to the NBA **Finals**. They beat the Phoenix Suns. Antetokounmpo became an NBA **champion**. He was chosen as the Finals MVP.

2021 NBA Finals MVP

TIMELINE

— 2011 —
Antetokounmpo plays club basketball in Greece

— 2013 —
Antetokounmpo is drafted by the Bucks

— 2017 —
Antetokounmpo is voted Most Improved Player

— 2019 —
Antetokounmpo wins his first MVP award

— 2021 —
Antetokounmpo wins the NBA championship and is the Finals MVP

LOOKING TO THE FUTURE

Antetokounmpo is a hero both on and off the court. He and his brothers started AntetokounBros. This basketball and education program gives kids the skills to grow.

Antetokounmpo loves the city of Milwaukee. He hopes to continue playing for the Bucks for many years. He plans to work hard to win more championships with the Bucks!

GLOSSARY

All-Star Game—a game between the best players in a league

blocks—plays made to stop an opponent's shot from going into the basket

champion—a winner of a contest that decides the best team or person

club—a basketball program that players advance through

defenders—players who try to stop the opposing team from scoring

draft—a process during which professional teams choose high school and college players to play for them

dribble—to bounce a basketball on the floor

Finals—the championship series of the National Basketball Association

most valuable player—the best player in a year, game, or series; the most valuable player is often called the MVP.

National Basketball Association—a professional basketball league in the United States; the National Basketball Association is often called the NBA.

power forward—a player who often plays close to the basket and is skilled at rebounding

rebounds—when players take control of basketballs after missed shots

rookie—related to a first-year player in a sports league

TO LEARN MORE

AT THE LIBRARY

Chandler, Matt. *Giannis Antetokounmpo: Basketball Powerhouse*. North Mankato, Minn.: Capstone Press, 2020.

Stabler, David. *Meet Giannis Antetokounmpo*. Minneapolis, Minn.: Lerner Publications, 2023.

Whiting, Jim. *The Story of the Milwaukee Bucks*. Mankato, Minn.: Creative Education, 2023.

ON THE WEB

Factsurfer.com gives you a safe, fun way to find more information.

1. Go to www.factsurfer.com

2. Enter "Giannis Antetokounmpo" into the search box and click 🔍.

3. Select your book cover to see a list of related content.

INDEX

All-Star Game, 16, 17
AntetokounBros, 20
awards, 16, 17, 18
blocks, 7, 16
champion, 18, 21
childhood, 8, 9, 10, 11, 12, 13
draft, 14
family, 8, 10, 13, 20
favorites, 9
Finals, 18
future, 21
Greece, 6, 8, 13
map, 15
Milwaukee Bucks, 4, 6, 7, 15, 16, 18, 21
Most Valuable Player, 16, 17, 18
National Basketball Association, 6, 7, 13, 14, 15, 16, 17, 18
nickname, 6
Nigeria, 8
power forward, 6
profile, 7
rebounds, 7, 16
records, 7, 15
rookie, 15
soccer, 8, 9
timeline, 18–19
trophy shelf, 17

The images in this book are reproduced through the courtesy of: Jeff Chiu/ AP Images, front cover (hero); Ververidis Vasilis, p. 3; Al Bello/ Getty Images, pp. 4, 4-5; Stacy Revere, pp. 6, 6-7; University of College, p. 7 (Bucks graphic); Aurelien Meunier/ Getty Images, p. 8; Aurelien Meunier - PSG/ Getty Images, p. 9; dean bertoncelj, p. 9 (football team); Nataliia K, p. 9 (food); Elena11, p. 9 (color); Tinseltown, p. 9 (actor); Michael Kovac/ Getty Images, p. 10; Mariano Garcia/ Alamy, p. 11; Nick Laham/ Getty Images, p. 12; REUTERS/ Alamy, p. 13; Mike Stobe/ Getty Images, p. 14; McClatchy- Tribune/ Alamy, p. 15; Tony Savino, p. 15 (Milwaukee, Wisconsin); 3brothers1sister/ Wiki Commons, p. 15 (Athens, Greece); Kevork Djansezian/ Getty Images, p. 16; Joe Scarnici/ Getty Images, p. 17; Jonathan Daniel/ Getty Images, p. 18; Milwaukee Bucks/ Wiki Commons, p. 18 (2013); Keith Allison/ Wiki Commons, p. 19 (2017); Jonathan Daniel, p. 19; Timothy Hiatt/ Getty Images, p. 20; Bob Levey/ Getty Images, p. 21; Erik Drost/ Wiki Commons, p. 23.